Talk

Michael J. Bugeja

The University of Arkansas Press
Fayetteville 1997

Manufactured in the United States of America

01 00 99 98 97 5 4 3 2 1

⊗ The paper used in this publication meets the minimum requirements of the American National Standard for Permanence of Paper for Printed Library Materials Z39.48-1984.

Designed by Alice Gail Carter

Library of Congress Cataloging-in-Publication Data

Bugeja, Michael J.
Talk / Michael J. Bugeja
p. cm.
ISBN 1-55728-471-7 (cloth : alk. paper). —
ISBN 1-55728-472-5 (paper : alk. paper)
I. Title.
PS3552.U387T3 1997
811'.54—DC21 91-15753
CIP

For Josephine Bugeja

(1921–1994)

Acknowledgments

These poems have appeared in the following journals:

The Formalist	"Burial," "Biological Clock," and "Lament of the Land-Grant Professor"
Hellas	"New Age," "Girl Talk," "Man Talk," and "Woman Talk"
The Lyric	"EPT"
The Nebraska Review	"The Talk"
Negative Capability	"Ars Poetica: The Influence of Lady Mary Wroth"
Plains Poetry Journal	"Gossip"
Poetry	"Trinity"
Prairie Schooner	"Baby Talk," "Love Talk," and "Body Talk"
Re: Artes Liberales	"Brainchild" and "Prayer"
The Sewanee Review	"Boomerang" and "The Influence of William Carlos Williams" under the title of "Dr. Williams Calls"
Sparrow	reprint of "Ars Poetica: The Influence of Lady Mary Wroth"
Spoon River Poetry Review	"The Land-Grant Professor Appeals for Sabbatical, Citing the Real Reasons"

Contents

Talk

What common language to unravel?

—WILLIAM CARLOS WILLIAMS

Spare me, then, till I am myself, and blessed . . .

—LADY MARY WROTH

The Talk

They have to have one on this walk
  In fields of the displanted,
Behind the trailer rows, cash crop:
  He has not yet been granted

A divorce or even filed for it,
  Hiding in Dakota bluffs
As an outlaw hides, bluffs, escapes.
  He can reinvent himself

Here the way he would in fiction:
  Bachelor meets strawberry blond
Still unaware of her beauty,
  Establishes lasting bond.

She has fallen in love and wants—
  This part is incredible—
To bear and care for his children;
  As yet, though, he's unable

To reveal the truth about his
  Estranged wife in Michigan
Who abandoned him years ago.
  It seems each time he begins

To say those words, looking at her
  Red lips, blue eyes, white skin—
So American, she could be
  Fine hand-painted porcelain—

He chokes and changes the subject,
  Grows quiet, withdraws, curses
Under his breath, averts his eyes.
  This is how bigamy occurs,

Not an act of selfishness but
  Cowardice, not an act of
Avarice but silence, omission.
  He cannot lose such a love:

He knows he will never find it
  Again, walking hand in hand
In the open field, grasshoppers
  Like flung rice on the land

Parting on either side of them,
  Creating an aisle, the sun
Casting elongated shadows
  Ahead of them, an omen.

She is talking about dinner,
  Maybe they should bake some bread,
Uncork some wine, have a picnic,
  Or head directly to bed.

He slows down as she talks about
  Love-making, making it good
For him because he does for her,
  Cuddle as long as they could

Bear that closeness, intimacy.
  Enough, he collapses there
On his knees, as if proposing,
  So she smiles and strokes his hair,

Her cotton dress unbuttoning,
  Blowing in the evening breeze,
Sculpting her, the undulating
  Buffalo grass to her knees:

The pure image of the prairie,
  The way men here have proposed

For a hundred years to women
  In the same field, the same pose.

She is waiting for him to speak,
  To plead *Will you marry me?*
But instead he has to tell her,
  I am already married,

Letting the meaning of that phrase
  Sink in, those other four words.
Finally, she helps him stand up,
  Holds his hand and pulls him toward

Their trailer; she really wants to
  Bake bread, uncork that bottle,
And picnic by the Sioux River,
  Where tonight they will cuddle,

Because they fit so well, his knees
  In the slope of her slim calves,
His chest in the slope of her back,
  His flesh in all the enclaves

Of her flesh, as it was always
  Meant to be, as it will be.
She's happy that he has told her
  The truth, she was worried,

For a minute, that he was ill
  Or in trouble with the law—
No need to fret about this, though,
  Just tend to it please. She saw

The talk coming, actually,
  But since it has, wonders now
Whether there is anything else
  He thinks that she should know.

Baby Talk

How it smooths and liquefies Teutonic
So language like pan Teflon does not stick

On diphthong or umlaut. The metronome
Of meaning loses meaning, it becomes

Loose and human as *'olelo o Hawai'i.*
We speak in the diminutive key of *E.*

For a little while, we are girls and boys
Employing equal arias of joy

Like birdsong in our cradles, our strollers,
Our bibs. Then echolalia occurs,

And nothing is the same. We heed the harsh
Consonants of adulthood: *tsk* and *shh,*

Our elders' awkward saws of alphabet.
Fluency is infantile, we forget,

It bubbles the saliva—a brook of vowels
And syllables on a tongue's mossy shales.

Girl Talk

At the lodge pool, two ten-year-old girls swim
To the deep end. They half float on the rim

And pump small waves with their feet, their heads turned
As if to shut out the world. They have learned

That pen pals do not write back when they go home.
Too soon, they know, their dads or moms will come

And call them to their rooms. So this may be
The last time to talk with blue lips and see

How close they could have been. Oh yes! They like
The same foods, same shows, same games and their bikes

Are pink and Schwinn. Their friends at school are nice.
They drink hot tea with milk and Coke with ice.

They wisp and sing these words, so soft a tone,
It sounds more like the *plink plink* of a stone

Skipped on a lake than girl talk. Then they burst
Out of the pool, stand, smirk and dive headfirst.

Boy Talk

At the baseball tryout, all but one are boys.
The girl warms up alone but hears the noise,

Words really, punctuated by noise: *Awesome,*
Someone says, and the rest release a groan. *Home,*

Another says, and the rest yelp. Then one mouths,
Breast, and everyone hoots. These are the truths

That boys will learn to trust, meaning and sound;
But now the girl ignores them on the mound,

Taking signals from the coach: *curve.* She can raise
Her longer leg and lower ERAs,

ABs—no words, not even *win* anymore—
Only numbers: *two-point-two* or *oh-for-four.*

They make boy talk, but many will not make
The team. They collapse on the bench and speak

Whole sentences to each other in leather mitts,
As close to fluency as boyhood gets.

Man Talk

The session starts with the phrase *man to man,*
But one speaks. The other has to listen

Once these words are said, a contract at stake.
Someone is getting sacked and etiquette

Calls for quiet, the subject—theft, divorce,
Jessica, cocaine (whatever the source)—

On the agenda today. How quickly
A man saunters from the lavatory

Talking TD, NBA, RBI,
To his doom, IRS or FBI,

Abbreviated lexicons of men.
He gives two-week's notice (gets 5 to 10).

Stats metamorphose with one measly trip
To the pop machine. This is fellowship,

Brothers, a talk that will end eye to eye
In an office without soliloquies.

Woman Talk

Their husbands their lovers their paramours
With whom they have lain for years months hours

Do not say the right real important things
Or say them too late too soon too something

While she sleeps weeps dreams with for of someone else
To make him pay break down shut up jealous

Express true false repressed any feelings
Emotions ambitions innermost longings

Still unfulfilled at home at the condo
At the Hilton then maybe she can do

The impossible and save the marriage
The relationship the tryst the baggage

Packed unpacked partially packed one more chance
Last chance slim/fat chance let's divorce date dance

Be friends rivals exs items couples
See a therapist priest other people

Love Talk

No more lines of Shakespeare *wherefore art thous*
No more *shall compare* or *how I love thees*

But now a spouse or partner parts the lips
To ear or lobe and then espouses slips

The analysts attribute to the tongue
Like pen pet nick names advertisements songs

After which a man and woman mimic parts
TV bleating in the bedroom as it starts

She's his animated Winnie he her Pooh
He's Mister Rogers she his Miss McGoo

She likens him to network anchorites
He loves her till the end of *Guiding Light*

She can melt the iceman as he cometh
As he taketh her in Nikes just doeth

Just dialeth 1-900 Hotline darling
Just keepeth going and going and going

Body Talk

As long as the hair would be stroked mussed combed
Its silk wire bob run upon the abdomen

The nose anuzzle in the nether places
The underside of calves knees hips faces

The lips parting suckling rubbing the zones
The lobes the nipples the loins the breastbones

The neck gone limp lolling back to be held
Licked kissed caressed bitten blown on cradled

As one would cradle the groin in a palm
Weigh it grasp it soothe it with a balm

Then the arms may entwine open or block
Then the legs may entwine open or lock

The joining coming together bonding
Of two into one as in the beginning

When the fluent body spoke broke exclaimed
So we would know whence we came whence we came

Brainchild

Hind

Let us celebrate the cerebellum
In a ballade melodious as a lullaby
And interlock our limbs until we come
To accept fate or infertility.
Let the medulla make this child the way
It makes the lungs inflate so we can breathe
In unison, involuntarily.
Maybe then we will conceive.

Mid

Let us key the lobes of equilibrium
And sing about umbilicals, accompany
The chamber music of the cranium.
Or let the pons compose a symphony
Sans a conductor, so we may occupy
The seats of all-being and make-believe,
Left and right. If we exalt the nuclei,
Maybe then we will conceive.

Fore

Let us sculpt the thalamus and cerebrum
With palms and mold the primordial clay
In our own image, a mixed medium.
We can put our creations on display
And marvel at our motor and sensory
Powers. Even specialists will perceive
The marriage of art and anatomy
And maybe then we will conceive.

Stem

Inside the hemispheres of ecstasy
A brainchild is easier to achieve.
Let us link up the parts and prophesy:
Maybe then? Will we conceive?

Life Cycles

for Diane and Shane

I. Biological Clock

You still have time to plan. The day you do,
You lose a child, and a couple years remain.
So calendars are kept, and rendezvous.
The more you dream the less you feel the pain.

You lose a child, or a couple. Years remain.
They do not heal the wounds but dull the words.
The more you dream the less you feel the pain
At twilight when their voices rise like birds.

They do not heal the wounds but dull the words
Echoing from the playground down the street
At twilight. When their voices rise like birds,
You think you hear the patter of their feet

Echoing from the playground. Down the street
The parents summon tardy children home.
You think you hear the patter of their feet
Outside your door. But they never come.

The parents summon tardy children home
By name. The Jennifers and Jasons run
Outside your door. But they never come.
You resurrect a daughter or a son

By name. The Jennifers and Jasons run.
You're out of breath and pushing forty now.
You resurrect a daughter or a son
Until you drift asleep in afterglow.

You're out of breath and pushing forty now
So calendars are kept, and rendezvous,
Until you drift asleep in afterglow.
You still have time to plan the day. You do.

II. New Age

The issue's been decided. Celebrate,
The psychic says. She hates to be misled.
You stare at her in awe and speculate.
Who knows the omens flashing in her head?

The psychic says she hates to be misled.
She has a reputation to protect.
Who knows the omens flashing in her head?
Well, she's no fool and seldom incorrect.

She has a reputation to protect
Despite what you may think. *I know your kind*
Well. She's no fool and seldom incorrect.
She reads your palm but cannot read your mind

Despite what you may think. *I know you're kind,*
A loving man, she quips, *with much to learn.*
She reads your palm but cannot read your mind:
Another child? Your wife awaits her turn.

A loving man, she quips, *with much to learn.*
You stare at her in awe and speculate
Another child. Your wife awaits her turn.
The issue's been decided. Celebrate.

III. EPT

Later in life if you want to start over,
You mess up a kit and go back to the store.
Re-reading the label, you quickly discover
The eyedropper missing. You leave to buy more.

You mess up a kit and go back to the store.
This time the liquid is measured precisely,
Missing the eyedropper. You leave to buy more.
Doing the lab work yourself can be dicey.

This time the liquid is measured precisely.
A ring should appear in the mirror below.
Doing the lab work yourself can be dicey,
Your heart beating fast and your clock running slow.

A ring should appear in the mirror below
The vial on the vanity. Try not to botch it,
Your heart beating fast and your clock running slow.
Miracles happen—you just have to watch it,

The vial on the vanity. (Try not to botch it.)
Re-reading the label, you quickly discover
Miracles happen. You just have to watch it
Later in life if you want to start over.

IV. Gender

True: some of us don't like surprises.
At first, though, the sex seldom matters.
It's simple, the sages advise us:
Just dote on your sons or your daughters.

At first, though the sex seldom matters,
The childless would like to have both.

Just dote on your sons or your daughters.
Let doctors keep track of the growth.

The childless would like to have both.
The second one comes with a crisis.
Let doctors keep track of the growth.
So this time you ask what the sex is.

The second one comes with a crisis.
At home you have boxes of clothes.
So this time you ask what the sex is.
The doctors have more to disclose.

At home you have boxes to close.
True: sometimes the reason is given.
The doctors have more to disclose.
In the end, even they are forgiven.

True: sometimes the reason is given.
It's simple, the sages advise us.
In the end, even they are forgiven.
True: some of us don't like surprises.

V. Trimesters

You measure the months by the sound of machines.
Why, even the word has an amphibrach ring
Like peaks on a gynecological screen,

Attune to the blips and the beats and the dings.
Why, even the word has an amphibrach ring
When you're wheeled in the room on a gurney of hope,

Attune to the blips and the beats and the dings.
The first thing you feel is a steel stethoscope
When you're wheeled in the room on a gurney of hope.

You're hooked to an ultrasound, waiting to view.
The first thing you feel is a steel stethoscope;
The last, a big lens on your womb. Greasy blue,

You're hooked to an ultrasound, waiting to view.
The second trimester has passed, now the third—
The last, a big lens on your womb. Greasy blue,

You're strapped to a monitor. Two hearts are heard.
The second trimester has passed. Now the third.
Because of malpractice, they schedule a test.

You're strapped to a monitor—two hearts are heard—
But then the prognosis: *Your baby's distressed.*
Because of malpractice, they schedule a test

Like peaks on a gynecological screen.
But then the prognosis: *Your baby's distressed.*
You measure the months by the sound of machines.

VI. Gossip

Is what comes back as bad as what goes out?
The first trimester silence is your friend.
You question whom to tell or whom to doubt.
In time the hurt will heal and feelings mend.

The first trimester silence is your friend.
The narrative develops as you grow.
In time the hurt will heal and feelings mend.
What to withhold tomorrow, and what now?

The narrative develops. As you grow,
The next trimester colleagues are informed
What to withhold tomorrow and what now.
You say there is no need to be alarmed.

The next trimester colleagues are informed
You have to take an early leave of absence.
You say there is no need to be alarmed—
The final weeks are filled—you keep appointments.

You have to take an early leave of absence
Because of gossip, of which you disapprove.
The final weeks are filled. You keep appointments
And a secret, out of loneliness and love.

Because of gossip, of which you disapprove,
You question whom to tell or whom to doubt.
And a secret out of loneliness and love
Is what comes back as bad as what goes out.

VII. Delivery

A modern birthing room would seem a choir
Practicing the downbeats and caesuras,
Timing every breath, as you require,
According to the techniques of Lamaze.

Practicing the downbeats and caesuras,
The rhythms *who-who-hee* inside your head
According to the techniques of Lamaze.
You wheeze an arietta on the bed;

The rhythms *who-who-hee* inside your head.
The baby improvises in your womb.
You wheeze an arietta on the bed.
The heart is amplified, a metronome.

The baby improvises in your womb
Another rockabilly lullaby.
The heart is amplified—a metronome—
Intervals decrease, pains intensify:

Another rockabilly lullaby.
It cannot go on longer, nurses lie.
Intervals decrease, pains intensify.
Were music sweeter than a baby's cry!

It cannot go on longer—nurses lie!—
Timing every breath, as you require.
Were music sweeter than a baby's cry,
A modern birthing room would seem a choir.

Prayer

for my surviving children

Your missing siblings also bear your names,
The only hand-me-downs: no broken toys,
Loose corduroys, coats. No abandoned bikes,
Balls, dolls or roller skates. You have angels:

The time will come when you will run with them
In heaven as you did on earth. The mown
Grass is greener there and dew-pearled at noon.
Trees climb like ladders and no top limbs snap.

As they have, forgive me my trespasses:
The late-night bickering with your mother,
The unfair timeouts and too sharp rebukes
At the table. Absence at the table.

May they lead you out of temptation and
Deliver you from evil: the open
Door, the closed pool, the small and plastic part,
The large and desperate women and men

About whom I have warned you so often.
Pray for them, too, my children. Remember:
There is no kingdom, power or glory
Greater than love here now and forever.

Trinity

God

You have distinct dimensions. They are we:
Encyclopedias and alphabets
Of the Big Bang, exobiology,
Inhabitants on multitudes of planets.

Our light cannot escape your gravity.
The soul is linked to yours, a diode
Through which we must return as energy
Until we flare like red suns, and explode.

We try to reconstruct you with an ode
Or explicate your essence line by line.
We canonize commandments like a code
Etched within the DNA. If we're divine,

Composing simple poems, making rhymes,
Then what are others in this paradigm?

Son

Then what are others in this paradigm
If not superior? We're grains of sand.
You have a billion planets to command
With technologies that attained their prime
Before we left the alluvial slime
For land and land for trees and trees for land
Again. These chosen beings went beyond
The boundaries and laws of space and time

To greater meccas. What miracles do
They require? How many stars, their magi?
Who, their Pilate? When, their Armageddon?

Were we made in God's image and they too?
Do you save sinners on Alpha Centauri,
All the nebular rosaries of heaven?

Spirit

All the nebular rosaries of heaven
Are bound by the lace of your cosmic string.
The unifying force, interwoven
In the clockwork of space-time, is a spring.

One moment we live here and the next, there.
The universe has edges off of which
No one will fall. Because you're everywhere,
Its seam appears the same from every stitch.

The Father sparks the singularity.
We breed like godseed in the firmament.
The Son forgives so that eternity,
Your sole domain, becomes self-evident.

Together you complete the trinity.
You have distinct dimensions: they are we.

Sightings

They come on wheel or crutch to pray at Lourdes.
The millions set up camp along the walks.
They line the wells that lead to the resort,
Awaiting wonderment or mercy. Tales
About Saint Bernadette abound. Her heels
Engrave the stone where Mary first appeared.

Today in town a rainbow arch appears
On the horizon, sudden light at Lourdes,
And then is gone. The holy water heals.
You catch it as it drips upon the walks
In magic pools or mop it up in tails
Of blouse or handkerchief. At the resort,

Inside chalets, the Jesuits re-sort
Accounts of cures, deciding which appear
Miraculous, divine, or fairy tale.
The verdict of the Vatican still lords.
It doesn't matter that a woman walks
Among the paralytic hordes and heals.

The pilgrims flock, then scatter on the heels
Of other sightings. As a last resort,
They dip their fingertips in bowls and woks
And cross their brows. They have to hike up here
To witness Mary manifest at Lourdes.
Her silken hood is white, her robe is teal;

The scent of roses, one more telltale
Sign. She is always silent when she heals.
And people always hail her with the Lord's
Prayer on their lips. She won't resort
To larger acts of awe. When she appears,
It is enough for those who see her walk

To revel in her spectra. Then all walks
Of life depart with parable or tale
Of how a vice or vision did appear,
Of how they healed or later could not heal,
Of how they ended up at a resort
And saw or did not see the Light at Lourdes.

She walks on mist, not water, as she heals
Mortality. The tale at the resort
Appears to be: *You make your peace at Lourdes.*

The Virgin Appears on Eyewitness News

She wearies the Vatican, missing as icon
In the papal church, above the candelabras;
Midnight the mobile unit turns its mike on,
Channeling audio abracadabras.

The anchor in the studio makes faux pas,
Happy talk to hype the phenomenon;
Advertisements ease the flus and the blahs.
She wearies the Vatican, missing as icon,

Correspondents say, and soon may abandon
The Urals, Lourdes, and Yugoslavias;
She won't reveal herself to priest or nun
In the papal church above the candelabras,

Nor appear in shady pools of shangri-las.
Instead she blesses parks in Oregon
Or picks a bath and spa in Arkansas.
Midnight the mobile unit turns its mike on

The milling crowds. The TV spotlights stun.
Someone sees a halo—hallelujahs!—
And cameras pan the sky in unison,
Channeling audio abracadabras.

Townsfolk come to feast on fish and slaw as
Venders peddle pizza, boxed communion;
The anchor at the station smiles and pauses,
Signing off as if he knows the reason
She wearies the Vatican.

The Conversion of Uncle Lucifer

It all comes back: the iron fence
  And rising steps of the church
Where Mother points out my bald
  And mythic arch-uncle. I search

The towering heads of the mob
  Bobbing as if they agree,
Placing blame where it belongs.
  Grandpa died, he has left me

The house and set up a trust.
  I miss him but am too young
To be taken seriously
  Among immigrants, my tongue

Unable to enounce my own
  Maltese name or decipher
The meaning of my mission,
  Converting Uncle Lucifer.

They say that I resemble him:
  I have heard Mother confess
The important comparisons
  About my future success,

So simple in America.
  I remember this climbing
Awkwardly upward in loafers,
  And campanile bells chiming

As Uncle analyzes me
  Atop steep cobblestone stairs,
Folding his arms in defiance.
  I'm nothing to him, an heir,

And he has a son to think of,
  My cousin with whom I may
Not play, and a native-born
  Wife to whom I may not say

Auntie or hello. I have learned
  These lessons like commandments
But must break them because Mother
  Wants to be loved and repents

Whatever she has done to him,
  Hoping he will see in me
Something beautiful, beggar child;
  He will call to her, take pity,

And she will be happy again.
  I stop halfway up the steps,
Halfway between them, and turn to
  Mother praying with pursed lips,

Closed eyes, rosary. I glance at
  Uncle, who has struck a stance
As if he wants to hear me out,
  Give Mother another chance

To redeem herself. I'll recite
  Her words like a psalm on cue
And drum them somehow in his head:
  My mother says she loves you.

I approach the open church door,
  And wheeze that to my uncle
Who bends down to me and replies:
  Tell your mom to go to hell.

Then he goes inside, vanishing
  In shadows as demons vanish,

So much as closing the church door,
  As if he would banish

My mother and me from refuge.
  I have to report to her,
Back down each difficult stone step,
  Saying that awful answer:

Go to hell. But she is gone too;
  She doesn't need to hear it,
Leaving me alone with those words,
  The power I inherit,

Realizing their prophecy:
  I succeed as everyone
Said I would in the family,
  But at their expense. I won

My place in the Maltese annals,
  The immigrant hierarchy,
But lost my innocence, Uncle,
  Your resonant legacy;

So that now, even as I write,
  I envision how evil
You were and have to convert you,
  Exorcise you from my will.

Bus Crash: Rutherford, N. J.

We will it so and so it is past all accident.
—WILLIAM CARLOS WILLIAMS

Death has little meaning: at eight,
  I associate it with pets,
Plants, the still and aquariumed
  Hamster, the Easter violets

Wilting in the third grade window,
  Franklin School, 1960,
My first beautiful teacher, young,
  Brunette, alive. A fantasy

Transfiguring boys who fixate
  On her red lips and bosom,
Punning her Poe-like name, Lenore,
  Smelling the pungent perfume

She dabs on the nape between bells,
  The aroma of recess,
Stirrings of sexuality.
  Thinking of her, embarrassed,

I sample testers and buy Mother
  The same perfume at Rexall's
To wear on parent-teacher night,
  Accompany her down the hall,

My teacher greeting us, saying
  He's wonderful, wonderful,
My mother greeting her, saying
  I know. Lenore in lambs wool,

Crinoline, her figure as full
  As the underside of moons
Rising above me, her Avoned
  Lips as scintillant as spoons

Laid atop each other: she tells
  Our parents that she's engaged,
And because I don't yet know what
  The word means, I act my age,

Bursting into the class to play
  With my mates while the hour
Passes and the smell permeates
  The elements, wildflower.

My only memory, her perfume,
  The rest I have imagined,
Pushed out of me, pieced together
  Then as it might have happened:

She boards the bus at the corner
  By the crossing guard, heading
To Rutherford where she will live,
  Where she has planned a wedding.

The bus barrels down Stuyvesant
  Avenue out of Lyndhurst
To the intersected Ridge Road
  Where Dr. Williams, immersed

In the sorry facts of his life,
  Composes mortal poems
In the dim lamplight of his den.
  The clock ticks, a metronome

In the moments before the crash.
  The bus outside his window

Illuminates his north room
  A brighter shade of yellow:

The broadsided hydraulic doors
  Unable to open, welded
Shut as the metal shears like foil,
  Passengers trapped or propelled

Out of seats to the curb, aflame,
  The doctor agape at his desk
Witnessing the spectacle, horror,
  The aftermath, the grotesque

Wailing of the dying, and dead,
  His appearing on the scene,
Perhaps trying to help Lenore
  While the leaking gasoline

Ignites on the main boulevard,
  Perhaps standing back, knowing
She's already beyond his help,
  The inflammable world, blowing

Away like violets out a window.
  The bridegroom weds another,
The boys burrow in the perfumed
  Lambs wool of weeping mothers,

And the sorrier Dr. Williams
  Returns to his study alone
To record the causes of death,
  Medical and melodic ones.

These, the desolate dark weeks
  Of a suburban M.D.
Who saves some people twice: at birth
  And middle age, with poetry,

So death still has little meaning.
  I associate it with metaphor:
The canonized, the forgotten,
  The still sweet scent of Lenore.

Burial

The stalks of wheat appear to writhe and bow
As funnel clouds descend upon the plain.
The farmer ends his dreaming with a plow.

The sirens in the village always blow,
As if to synchronize his life of pain.
The stalks of wheat appear to writhe and bow

Then burst into a thunderclap of crow.
They flap against sky but do not gain.
The farmer ends his dreaming with a plow.

The funnel clouds increase, the shadows grow.
A gust of wind revolves the weather vane.
The stalks of wheat appear to writhe and bow.

His family beckons but he will not go
To shelter as the twister tills the grain.
The farmer ends his dreaming with a plow

To meet his fate in fields. He does not know
The apparitions bobbing in the rain.
The stalks of wheat appear to writhe and bow.
The farmer ends his dreaming with a plow.

Lament of the Land-Grant Professor

My Ph.D. was passed to me by a dean
Named Billie in a Big Eight stadium
On the Astroturf. I saw the future then.
My mentor mispronounced my Maltese name
And hooded me in the flamboyant silks
Of my ancestors—my colors, gilt and teal—
All the accouterments of academe
As I had dreamed of them in my boyhood,
Budding Giordano Bruno. Oh to teach
In towers of real ivy—Harvard, Princeton, Yale—
Or ones with gothic names: Bryn Mawr, Radcliffe!
Trustees would take arcane, exotic posts
As missionaries or ambassadors to Belize,
And no one would raise cattle or sink wells;
Tycoons who *poink* tobacco into goblets
Would not slap me on the back at barbecues.
My office would have two doors, one to class
In a room with stepped rows and marble floors,
One to the lobby where busts of Copernicus,
Kepler and Galileo appoint the walls.

My basement office leaks and has no windows,
And two of my colleagues have passed away
Because my legislature would not pay
To remove asbestos from the cracked ceiling.
(I eulogized them at their memorials
Without mentioning their melanomas.)
And the students, bless them, who cannot spell
Or punctuate when I get them, who believe
A baccalaureate is a work permit,
And a keg of cool beer, a rite of passage:
How to save them? Emeriti die here
The way salesmen do in Arthur Miller plays
As flunkies, and yet how few in his or her
Prime as professor would admit what I am

Now in my fortieth year, in full viropause,
Lamenting the waste of time and talent,
Becoming eccentric out of *echt* boredom,
Composing maudlin poems instead of
Maintaining my labs in a bleached cotton coat
As the ceiling flakes on my slumped shoulders?

Reply of the Land-Grant Professor Whose Hours Have Been Questioned

I know it's wrong to lump the lot of them,
To de-evolve blue collar men and women
To mere grease monkeys—oil pan troglodytes,
As it were—but one such primate in Muskogee
Composed a letter to the governor,
And life at A&M has gotten worse.
A mechanic complained about taxes and blamed academe.
I read an excerpt in the local paper.
They work a seven-hour week, he wrote,
And teach a couple classes! Once he saw
A prof mow lawn at 9 A.M.: *Proof enough!*
So cut our taxes, and their salaries!
The governor agreed. (He did not ask
The good mechanic why he was at home then.)

My desk is littered with a hundred papers
On fundamental forces. Dumbo physics.
I would like to mail them to mechanics,
Who by law require seven breaks a day,
To grade and then explain the many Fs
The way they do transmissions when they fail,
That surly grin, and answer to the dean
When angry parents telephone. My own
Mechanic father never knew why I
Would teach as long as Michigan made cars,
And high school oafs, who copied my exams,
All bought the heaps that he would fix and sell,
Or sell and fix, like this Muskogee man,
My nemesis, to whom I yield again.

The Land-Grant Professor Defends Tenure before the Legislature

Most of you are lawyers, private practice,
With precious little knowledge of big business;
But would apply its rules to academe.
What do you know of rules besides the ones
Professors taught you? You even took a test—
The bar—before we let you loose. Worse,
Your models come from Rome and Babylon.
Where would you be without books? Translations?
And what if dons at Harvard long ago
Refused to take you in, condone the discipline?
The system you assail created you.
We're close as kin. How would the ABA
Respond to resolutions limiting
The life appointment of a U.S. judge?

I'm a physicist and work with business.
(No bid is quite as cheap as academe's.)
The private sector also tenures when
It has to honor someone's severance pay.
It reassigns or transfers till he quits.
The more I work, the less I seem to earn
Because you fix my salary each year
Within this room. You take a cut when I
Consult, and patents out on my machines.
So colleagues criticize my energy.
The sweat that won me tenure early on
Would lose it now. You proved yourself, they say,
And make the rest of us look bad. Fact is,
I'm ethnic, and I don't know when to quit.
I fear someone will fire me. Maybe you.

The Land-Grant Professor Explains the System to His Therapist

I love it when my deans clip on lapels
Those patriotic pins, those mini flags,
So proud to be Americans (at least
At public functions with potential donors).
Perhaps the nouveau riche will feel a pang,
Endow a chair: The Joe Mechanic Seat
Of Auto Science. How they do pretend,
These new entrepreneurs of academe,
To run a college like a business!
The more they act like MBAs, the more
The regents listen: *Trim the fat! Tighten belts!*
Leaner days! (You'd think they were nutritionists
The way they carry on at budget time.)
And then the governor who wears a pin
On his lapel woos them at the mansion.

I call them academic socialists.
When times are good, so too the five-year plans.
When times are rotten, everyone is lousy.
The finer teachers earn as much as the bad.
The best and worst departments operate
On equal budgets. The so-called merit raise,
A token thousand dollars—divvied up,
Parceled out—is tantamount to turkeys
My mechanic dad received Thanksgivings.
No wonder I'm depressed. All those wasted
Years of trying to invent the perfect
Tool to shoot an isotope, implode it,
And only I implode. The governor,
To save the state, has cut my benefits,
So now I have to pay for therapy.

The Land-Grant Professor Fries His Annual Review

I used to read them, surly notes by chemists,
By and large, who rule the land-grant system.
They're in cahoots with the geologists.
Both rape the Earth. The chemist bakes a dust
For crops here till the dirt cannot be tilled;
Geologists can drill it then. And when
The aquifers and fossil fuels are gone,
Tycoons and companies renege on grants.
It puts my colleagues in the foulest mood
(Except the new biologists who patent
Mutant plants for the desert-like terrain).
I would put the chemists out of business
But nuclei will not fuse and self-sustain.
Like hope, they flare awhile and flicker out.
My engines burn more fuel than they generate.
The argument against me goes like this:
Every test's a failure, and so are you.

When I arrived to teach at A&M,
The aquifers and wells were at the prime.
A subatomic physicist made sense
The same way poets do in academe:
Impress alumni. It never works, of course.
The physicist and poet, Don Quixotes
On a quest, realize the others base
Their disciplines on molecule or myth.
So colleagues pop our bubbles in reviews.
No money is involved, no merit pay—
We split it like a pie amongst ourselves—
And I, already tenured, have attained
The title of full prof. So why the fuss?
I take my letters to the lab and light
A Bunsen burner. Chemists like me now—
They even say hello—and all I lose,
Besides the stress, is my sense of purpose.

The Land-Grant Professor Comforts an Untenured Assailant in the Parking Lot of Piggly Wiggly

It was dusk. A dark-complected man was bobbing
Up and down on the driver side of your Celica.
What else were you to think besides a theft?
Of course it seemed that I was picking locks
Instead of loading sacks of groceries
On the passenger seat of a beat-around Buick.
I wish you hadn't spun me from behind
And called me *wop*—I'm actually Maltese
But have been spun before and labeled worse.
I doubt you know my archipelago
Between the continent of Africa
And Sicily. If this had happened there,
I'd have to kill you on the spot or lose
Respect. (I'm only joking, naturally.)
You're not the first white Anglo-Saxon male
To err, if that makes any difference.
I shop here after class in suit and tie,
And patrons always ask about the products,
Assuming I'm the manager. I tell them

I'm a physicist, full prof. My only goal
So far in life is fusion, melding nuclei,
Bringing them together, much like people:
Me and you. Only first they must collide,
As we have done today, to overcome
What science calls *repulsion*. I'll clarify.
You saw me near your car and felt repulsed,
Accelerated toward me in your Nikes.
The closer you came, the stronger you felt
Repelled by my appearance. After all,
I was armed with tool or blade to steal
Your Celica and still the energy
Inside you welled and burst. It self-sustains.

You're weeping on your knees at Piggly Wiggly.
You're apt to feel a bond for many years.
Rest assured, I want to shoot an isotope—
Not you, a mere associate—to trigger that
Reaction in the lab. Now tell me, when,
Exactly, do you plan to ask for tenure?

The Land-Grant Professor Appeals for Sabbatical, Citing the Real Reasons

You know my research well. For many years,
With certain glee, you've seen experiment
Upon experiment accelerate
And bomb inside the lab. No loss to you.
The private sector sponsored all my tests
To shoot an isotope, and though I failed,
Methods of a failure are important.
My contribution lies in saving time.
A physicist eliminates until
He happens on the right hypotheses.
It's hypocritical, denying this
Appeal, maintaining I will flop again.
Admit it: Do you want me to succeed?
Imagine megabucks, publicity,
My name and mug (not yours) appearing on
The covers of your favorite magazines:
Newsweek, Nature, Science, Man of the Year
In *Time.* I'd be a guest on Larry King,
Answering your calls. Could you cope with that?

Of course not. Time has come to tell the truth.
You want me on sabbatical because
You will not see me in the lab or hall.
I will cast no vote in your committees,
Compose no snarky letters to the dean
About the influence of chemists on
Curricula or the purchase of equipment.
Think of it: Geologists on field days
Sinking oil wells where species used to roam.
Biologists may mutate what remains—
The corn will taste like foam, the pork like string—
But I won't be around to sound the warning.
No, I'll be somewhere else—and that's the point.

Maybe on a slow boat bound for Malta,
Maybe here, Muskogee, Oklahoma,
Inside a rented cabin by the lake.
I'll slate my nervous breakdown. Best of all,
It won't occur at class. I'll spare you that
If you will let me keep my dignity.

Ars Poetica: The Influence of Lady Mary Wroth

A crown of sonnets—
In this strange labyrinth how shall I turn?

I. Epigram: To the Earl of Pembroke

Will not thy rage be satisfied with this?

My sonnet is more lethal than your sword.
My feather has a sharper point. You dip it
In a vial of poison ink and sip it
Up as ears do gossip. You say you heard
Talk of my treason among the many lords
At court who fear a confessional poet,
Discovered my scribbles in the closet,
Exposing the king to ridicule. One word,

You warn, and you shall inform James the First,
Who also loves a sonnet. In the tower
I can immortalize Scots on the throne,
Or abdicate to you in bed. Lips pursed,
Tapping my heel to the pentameter,
I'm memorizing sestets till you're done.

II. Warning: To the Earl, Her Cousin

If lust be counted love 'tis falsely nam'd . . .

I'm memorizing sestets till you're done,
Completing what you started in the bed.
The latest sonnet echoes in my head
As you profess your love. I let it drown

Your sorry proclamations—you'll atone—
And now betray the libel you have said
In my presence about the late beheaded
Catholic queen whose son converts a throne.

In time the king will lead us to the same
Bloody stump as half our heirs. I am kin!
You do not talk of love but lust and took
What noblemen protect, a widow's name.
You took far more than that, unkind cousin.
Recite me now, and you recite your book.

III. Apology: To Uncle Philip

There came to my remembrance a vanity
wherein I had taken delight . . .
—SIDNEY'S FINAL CONFESSION

Recite me now, and you recite your book,
Dear Brave Bulleted Uncle Philip. Misled
By your *Defence of Poesie,* I read
Your arguments with girlhood glee, mistook
Your talk of Eros as to me and undertook
To base my poetry on the purebred
Theme of benighted love. Such love is dead.
You see it in the eyes of earl and duke

When noblemen invoke your name at court.
They cannot rouse the king or rob his purse
As you did vain Elizabeth. They cannot
Appease him with apologies or thwart
Their enemies with elevated verse.
They march to meter, rhyme to counterplot.

IV. Masque of Blackness

Better are they who thus to blackness run . . .

They march to meter, rhyme to counterplot,
The knights who saw us masque, to mask the night.
We shadowed ladies danced to candlelight,
Delighting in the deeper shades. We forgot,
For a little while on stage, our clotted
Bloodlines of spouse, paramour, parasite.
We moved freely as Moors or nomads might,
Our bodies and faces blackened with soot.

The king enjoyed himself, watching women
Painted and still panting in their costumes,
Bow down to him. He talked about that theme.
Later, when we soaped and scrubbed our skin,
More rosy than white, his men would consume
Cups of ale and wine, continue to blaspheme.

V. Song: To Ben

Drink to me only with thine eyes,
And I will pledge with mine . . .
—FROM JONSON'S "SONG: TO CELIA"

Cups of ale and wine continue to blaspheme
My role at court. When drunken bouts begin
To undermine me, I can discipline
Crueler than a man. I'm not what I seem,
A widow in the Earl of Pembroke's home.
He talks of us at masques. The guise is thin,
Insiders say. You solicit him as patron,
But he suspects that "Celia" is my name.

Do not reveal my real one and sober up.
Cease using similes of drink and death
To symbolize the love you claim for me.
Stop looking for my kisses in a cup
And likening red roses to my breath.
I wouldn't get that close, Ben. Take pity.

VI. Warning: To the Drunken Playwright

What pleasure can a banish'd creature have?

I wouldn't get that close. Ben, take pity
On yourself instead of me. You invite
My rage, not my patronage, when you write
Poems and dedicate your plays to me.
You talk of me as *woman* or as *lady.*
Such titles don't entitle but affright,
And I must lose them to attain the height
That I have set within my coterie.

Compare your influence to mine. I'll sing
So loud of your abuse, the king shall ban
Your comedies and cage you like a dove.
The truth is that I know you're suffering
As you deserve. But you'll suffer again
To pen more verse, indicting me of love.

VII. Another Warning

I that have been a lover, and could show it,
Though not in these, in rhymes not wholly dumb,
Since I exscribe your sonnets, am become
A better lover, and much better poet . . .

—FROM JONSON'S "A SONNET,
TO THE NOBLE LADY,
THE LADY MARY WROTH"

To pen more verse indicting me of love!
Then to pun my sonnets as your teacher
And my title twice in yours! You butcher
Poetry to make it. Your slow rhymes rove
Like lurid eyes over the corpus of
My passion and your thumpety meter
Bores my ears like talk. You're but a fixture
Now before me, a sty I must remove.

Fact is, when you close your eyes you see me.
When you stopper your ears, you hear my song
Tapping the inner drums of your muses.
You write a masque of blackness or of beauty
And cast a role for me to woo the king.
The woman you would use also uses.

VIII. Yet Another

Good now be still, and do not me torment . . .

The woman you would use also uses
Weapons at her disposal to expel
Men who hem her at the Pembroke table.
She has forked deer hearts here and kicked bruises
With the toe horn of a boot. She confuses
Repartee for back talk, knives for scalpels,
And won't play Stella to your Astrophel
Nor listen to your iambs of excuses.

She has abandoned the arts of apology
And embraced the sciences of torment.
She'll play you as Cupid plays the lute.
Be still, or you shall hear your elegy
At court. The sonnet is her instrument.
This lady aims her quill and executes.

IX. Elegy: To Her Late Husband

Think then your will, and left, leave me yet more . . .

This lady aims her quill and executes
Your testament. The sum that you bequeath
King James is more of your abuse. Even death
Alas in England cannot stop a brute
Who leaves a widow, bruised and destitute,
To the whims of court. You consumed my youth.
My father hung me on you like a wreath
Upon a grave. I will resurrect, uproot

The romance of an unromantic age.
The earls will analyze my lines anew
And liberate my swallows like a hawk.
I will spill rivulets of verse on the page
As men spill blood on snow, and malign you,
My dead indecent master. *Lord, I will talk.*

X. Epistle: To the King

Implore not heaven, nor deities,
They know too well his forgeries . . .

My Dear and Decent Master: Lord, I will talk
About my estate and bid your help today.
Debts mount, I dwell with kin. To my dismay
I cannot come to court when men provoke

My wrath and women sneer behind my back.
I plead my case with pen and ink, convey
Apologies, and ask that you defray
Loans my husband left to me. Out of wedlock,

I cannot pay my creditors and risk
My widowed coat of arms. I feel defiled.
The only labor I anticipate
Employs a bed and afterward my desk
To write my masterwork. I am with child
Whose father is the broker of my fate.

XI. Lament: To the King

Let not his falsehood be esteemed
Least your self be disesteemed . . .

Whose father is the broker of my fate?
What man becomes the agent of demise?
What dashing uncle dashes dreams with lies?
Which eager cousin comes to procreate
The next in line? Which poet laureate
Convinces me that I should compromise?
What king awards a woman like a prize
And asks her to submit to his mandate?

So I will keep his house, but not his name.
So I will raise his heirs, but not his hopes.
So I will cede my body, but not my worth.
So I will forfeit love, but not acclaim.
So I will cease my talk, but not my tropes.
So I will lose my head, but not my truth.

XII. Letter: To the Libeled Lord Denny

I never thought of you in my writing . . .

So I will lose my head. But not my truth:
The facts differ, my doubtful Lord Denny.
First, the simple matter of names: Do I
Disclose your own, or in-law son's, or both?
The reason for your beaten daughter's death,
Dearest honest Honora? Or identify
Those who'd indict her of adultery?
The evidence is neither above nor beneath

Your checked and checkered life. It's parallel:
I never thought of you in my writing
But Honora, whose pain pained me to such extent,
I had to talk for her. If there's libel,
It's what I have withheld. So tell the king
The facts are wrong. Produce your documents.

XIII. Penance: To the King

Let not them fear . . . what my blood calls me
to be and what my words have said me to be . . .

The facts are wrong. Produce your documents
Indicting me. I'm banished anyway.
Invite me back to hear what others say
About my book. In any case I sent
My servants here and on the continent
To confiscate all copies and repay
Nobles who have bought them. Without delay,
You may assail or silence me. I repent,

A candid woman, who talks and ridicules
Your men so awesome in their iron coats.
They serve as soldier, knight, or diplomat,
Protect your castles, legislate your rules,
Command your armies, commandeer your boats.
I thought a man was mightier than that.

XIV. Promise: To the Earl of Pembroke

Gods do princes hands direct,
Then to these have some respect . . .

I thought a man was mightier than that,
My sullen earl. Did you dissolve your will
To learn I was bequeathed to you but still
Not yours to tether like a common cat?
I purr to bear your heirs. My habitat
Becomes a bed within your domicile.
I will go down loving you, not the aisle;
I will never talk of marriage nor combat

Your appetites. So have your way with me.
I promise to conceal your impotence
Before the king. I will give you my word,
My body, my babies, and my pedigree,
But not my poetry. Make no pretense:
My sonnet is more lethal than your sword.

Note

The epigraphs in this crown of sonnets are adapted from Elizabethan variations as found in *The Poems of Lady Mary Wroth,* edited by Josephine Roberts (Baton Rouge: Louisiana State University Press, 1983). Roberts has an informative introduction about Wroth's life; these facts I varied in my crown. For instance, we don't know for certain that Ben Jonson was obsessed with Wroth, but he seemed to be obsessed with a certain "Celia"—whom I think is Wroth. Moreover, Jonson dedicated his most famous play, *The Alchemist,* and three poems of admiration to Wroth. She was born Mary Sidney in 1586 or 1587 and was the niece of Sir Philip Sidney, who wooed the poet-queen Elizabeth I with his verse; but the court of James I was more cynical about the arts. Poetry and platonic love fell from favor. Mary Sidney's marriage to an older man, Robert Wroth, was unhappy; when he died, he left her deeply in debt. Her first cousin William Herbert, earl of Pembroke and a patron of Shakespeare and Jonson, had a relationship with Wroth, who bore him two children. There is some evidence to suggest that Pembroke was a sexual opportunist, and I cast him as such in the poem, although it is possible that literary myth is correct and Lady Mary Wroth was smitten by his good looks. (This seems out of character.) Her sonnets did not get her into trouble with Sir Edward Denny, a violent man, but her mammoth prose romance *Urania* did because it was based in part on actual events at court. Lord Denny did accuse her of libel. She, in turn, showed no fear of him and dashed off a poem that called him an "ass." In the end, she was required to recall her book in England and abroad on orders from the Duke of Buckingham, who acted on behalf of the king. For simplicity's sake, I allow her sonnets to enrage Lord Denny and have her deal directly with the king in my poem. Wroth died without many supporters at court in 1651 or 1653. All this is documented in letters that appear in *The Poems of Lady Mary Wroth,* a book I highly recommend for anyone interested in Wroth's life, works, or how she executed the sonnet crown.

The Influence of William Carlos Williams

He cannot help this time. I am to blame,
Dreaming of the dead physician-poet,
Immortal lines within a story frame
Inside the office of his old estate

On 9 Ridge Road in Rutherford. I'm eight:
He's swabbing me with cotton, arm aflame;
I watch him push the needle in, and wait:
He cannot help this time. I am to blame,

Drawing on his influence, mere phantasm,
As he draws blood from me, inoculates
Against the influenzas of acclaim.
Dreaming of the dead physician-poet,

I open envelopes and veins of fate
On the gurney. He listens to the iambs
Of my ordinary heart to demonstrate
Immortal lines within a story frame.

He aims a penlight at the inner drum
Of my ear and shakes his head, irrigates
My tongue and then depresses it: inflamed.
Inside the office of his old estate,

My poems lie in piles. The doctor states
Prognoses candidly and puts the blame
On too much Milton, far too little Yeats,
On too much meter, an overdose of rhyme:
He cannot help this time.

Boomerang

Our lives are like pantoums. Those lines come back
To haunt us. Say your mantras, make your peace.
Every slur you heard is elegiac:
Something dies within. Something is released

To haunt us. Make your mantras, say your piece:
You were worthless then, dear. And worthless now.
Something dies within. Something is released.
In time you'll learn to let your goodness go—

You were worthless then, dear, and worthless now—
And concentrate on arts of pain instead.
In time you'll learn, too. Let your goodness go
To waste on every partner in your bed,

And concentrate on arts of pain. Instead
Of needing love, remember you have lines
To waste on every partner in your bed:
You disappoint me. You show all the signs

Of needing love, remember? You have lines
To undermine a person's getting close:
You disappoint me. You show all the signs.
If you're nothing, you have nothing to lose,

To undermine. A person's getting close.
Every slur you heard is elegiac.
If you're nothing, you have nothing to lose.
Our lives are like pantoums. Those lines come back.